Saint Julia

Through faith and purity, to Jesus Christ.

STORIES OF SAINTS FOR CHILDREN SERIES

10

Retold and illustrated by S.V. SBIERA

© 2023 S.V. SBIERA

Saint Virgin Martyr Julia of Carthage
July 16

3

One of the greatest gifts from God is the pure soul of every child born on Earth.

If someone has a pure soul, it means their soul is untainted or uncorrupted by all the bad things in the world. Angels also have this virtue, and it is highly valued by God.

Unfortunately, many children lose this virtue as they become adults and are exposed to the evils of this world. But some children remain pure and become adults pleasing to God. One example is Saint Julia. Let's discover her life together.

Almost five centuries after the birth of Christ, a young girl named Julia lived in the city of Carthage of the Roman Empire (today's Tunis in North Africa). Julia was raised in a noble Christian family, and she received a special education. Her parents loved her very much and taught her to pray and love Jesus.

7

When Julia was around ten years old, Persian soldiers attacked her city. They captured many children, including Julia, and sold them into slavery in Syria.

But God, in His infinite compassion, stood by Julia and gave her the strength to endure the cruel separation from her parents and keep her soul pure.

Julia's master, named Eusebius, was a pagan merchant. Since Julia was a Christian, Eusebius tried convincing her to renounce her faith with kind words. But he soon lost patience and started threatening her instead.

Julia answered him decisively, "I'd rather choose to die than give up Jesus!"

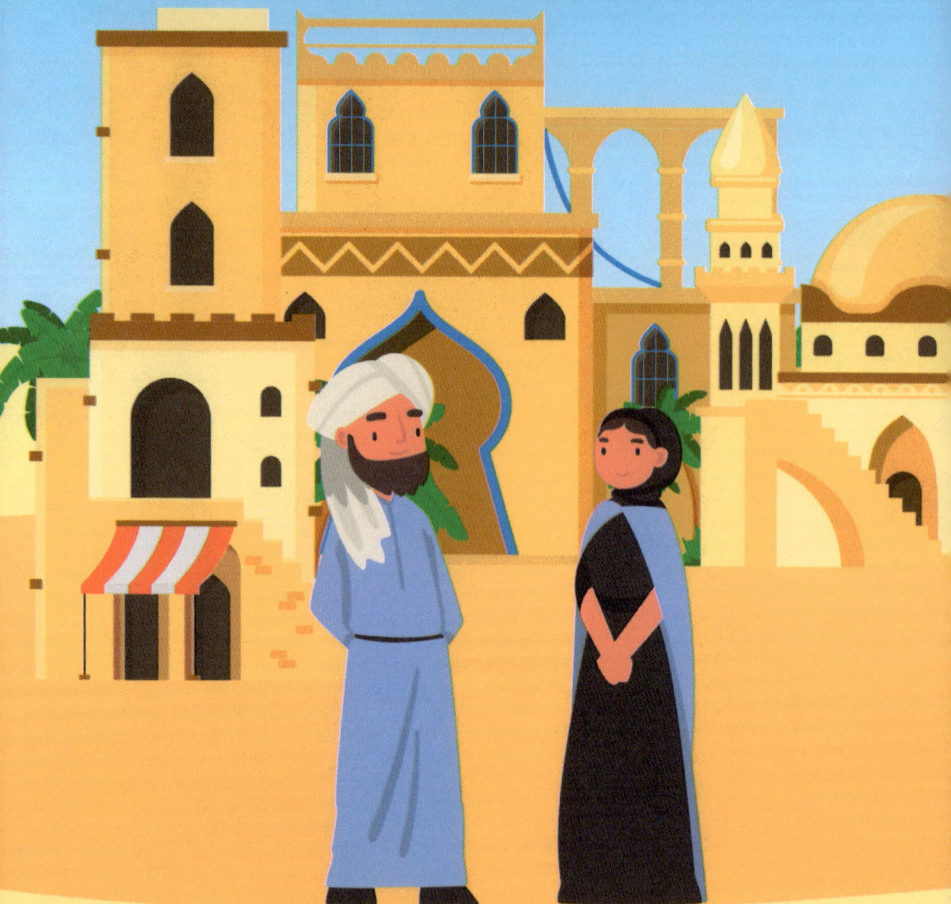

Although she was very young, Eusebius was impressed by her strong faith. Because Julia fulfilled her duties with great diligence, he gave up trying to convert her faith.

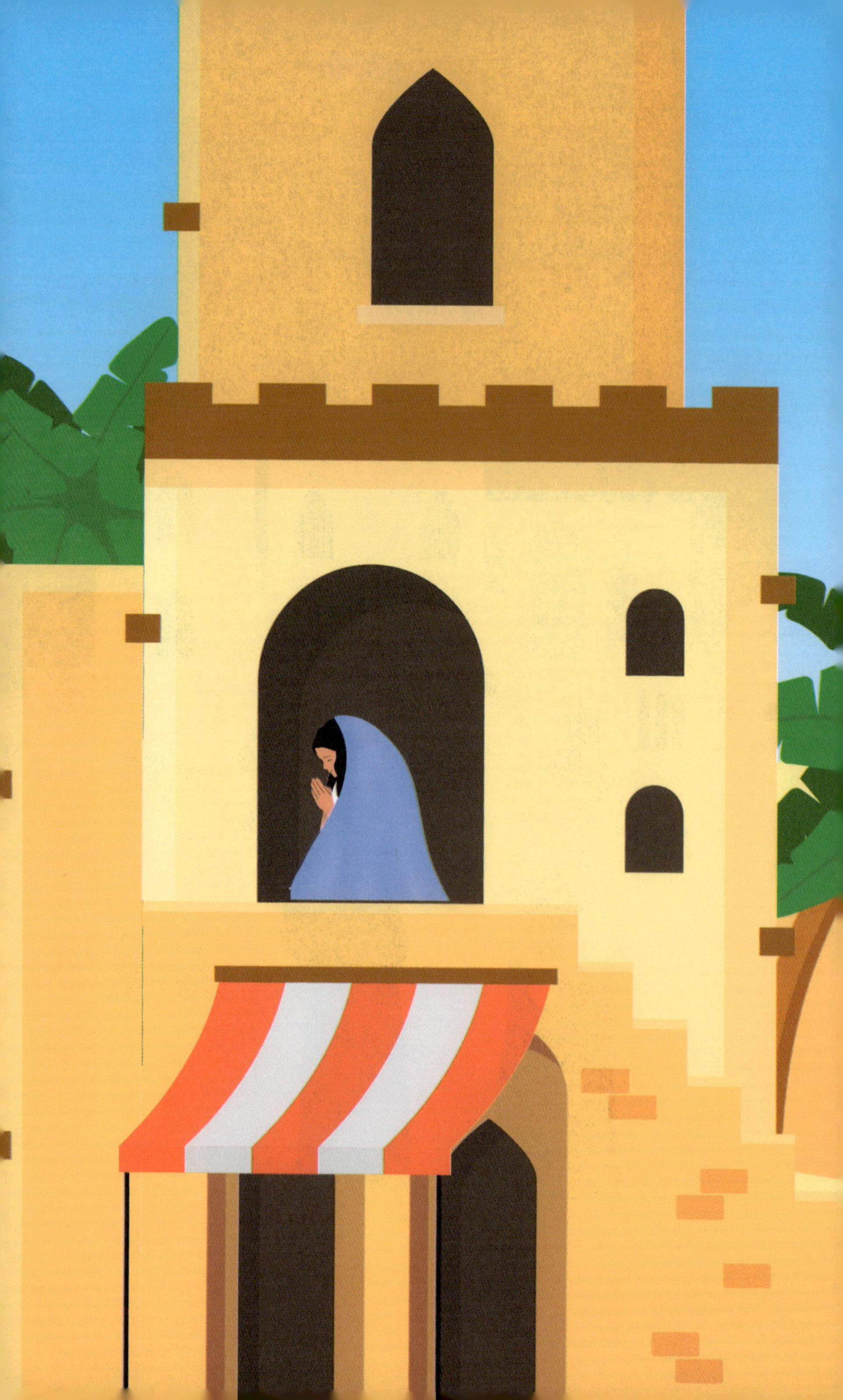

Ten years passed, and Julia faithfully served her master without complaint. Thanks to Julia, the wealth of Eusebius multiplied. She kept her soul pure all this time by fasting and praying to God. In her little free time, she read the scriptures.

Once, Eusebius set off with merchandise for Gaul and took Julia with him. Along the way, the ship stopped over at the island of Corsica. Eusebius decided to take part in a pagan festival, but Julia remained on the ship.

15

Eusebius bought a fattened calf and sacrificed it to the gods, rejoicing, eating, and drinking with the Corsicans. Julia sighed at their error.

17

One of the Corsicans saw Julia on the ship and told the pagan high priest about her.

The pagan high priest, called Felix, asked Eusebius: "Why isn't the girl on your ship attending the festival to worship our gods?"

"She is a Christian. I tried to convince her, but she would rather choose to die than give up her faith!" replied Eusebius.

"Give her to me, and I will give you four other handmaidens in return," demanded Felix.

"I will not give up Julia for anything. Thanks to her, my wealth has multiplied," Eusebius refused.

19

Felix pretended to accept Eusebius's refusal, but he soon hatched a cunning plan to kidnap Julia. The Corsicans made Eusebius and his companions drunk with wine until they fell asleep, then they took Julia from the ship.

21

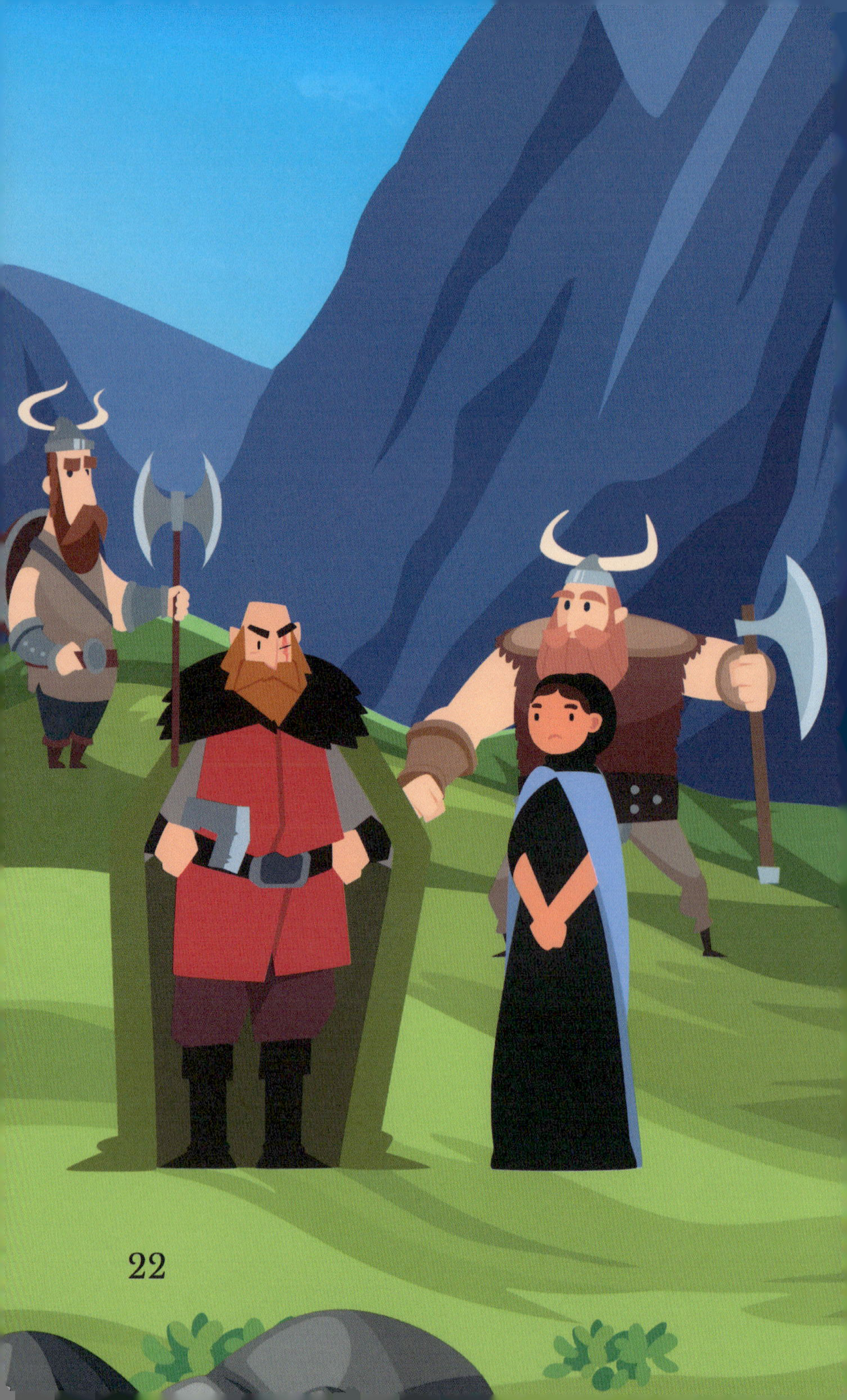

Brought before Felix by the raging mob, Julia was not afraid to admit that she was a Christian.

Felix said, "Sacrifice to the gods, girl, and I will give you your freedom!"

"My liberty is the service of Christ, whom I serve every day with a pure mind. As for that error of yours, I detest it," Julia replied boldly.

"You will be beaten if you don't obey," Felix sneered.

"If my Lord Jesus Christ endured beatings, humiliations, and a crown of thorns, then shall I not also endure these for Him?" answered Julia.

24

The pagans tortured Julia, but she bravely endured the torment because the Lord strengthened her. Seeing that nothing could shake Julia from her faith, the pagans crucified her like our Lord Jesus Christ.

When the soul of the Holy Martyr Julia left her body, all those present saw a snow-white dove flying from her mouth, and an angel of the Lord next to her. Terrified, they fled, leaving her body on the cross.

An angel of the Lord announced the death of Saint Julia to the monks of a monastery on a nearby island. The monks took the body of the saint and buried it with honor in the church of their monastery.

Miraculous healings began to take place at the tomb of St. Julia, and Christians from all over the world asked for the saint's help. Many testified about the miracles they received, thanking God and Saint Julia for it.

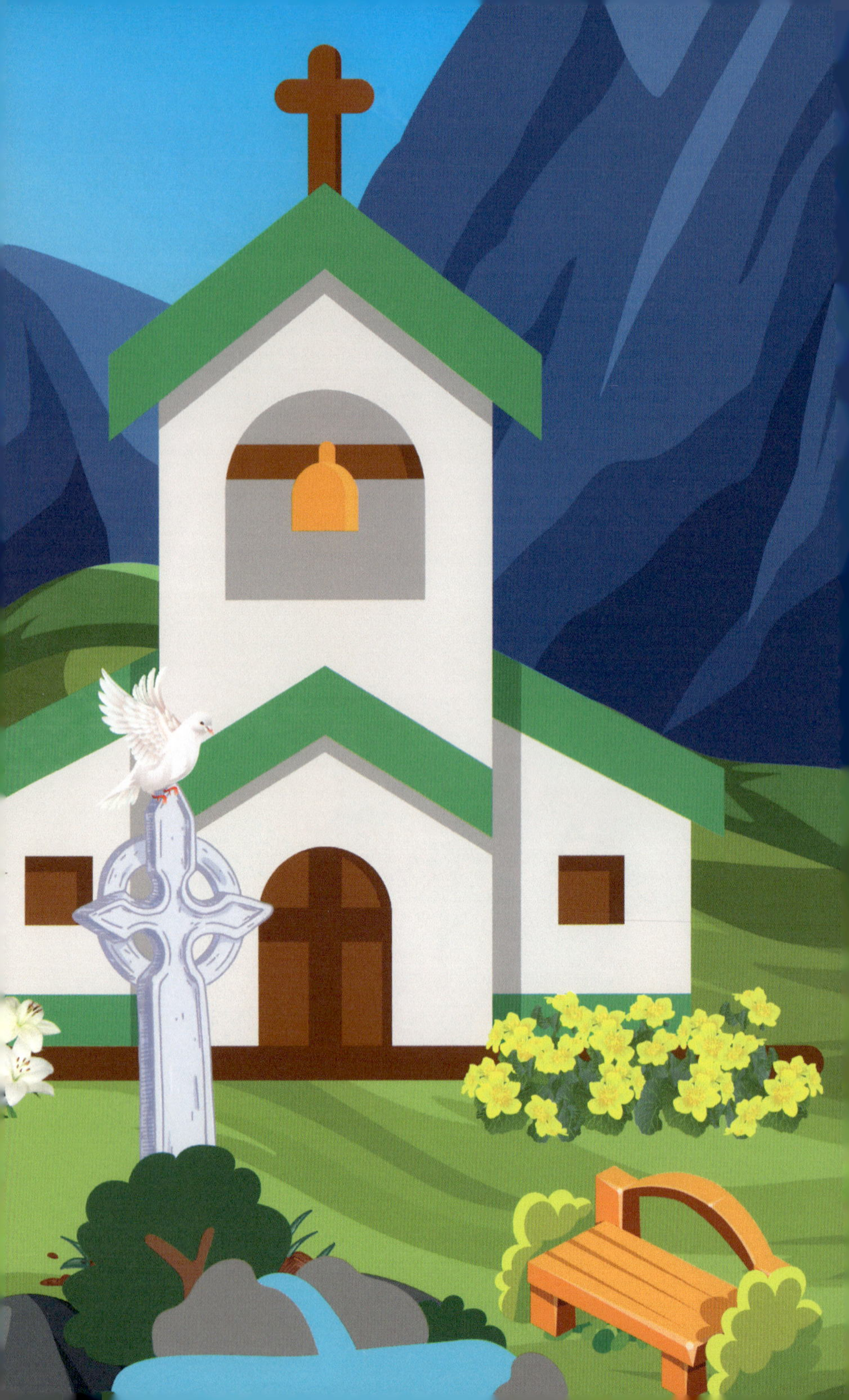

In the place where Saint Julia was crucified, a spring appeared. Those who drank water from the spring with faith were cured of diseases. Many Corsicans converted to Christianity and built a small church near the spring.

Later, when all the Corsicans became Christians, they considered Saint Julia the protector of the island of Corsica.

Today, many Christian families choose the name of Saint Julia for their daughters as a sign of honoring her or as a patron saint.

The life of St. Julia proves that we can reach heaven and be with Jesus Christ through faith and purity.

IN THIS SERIES

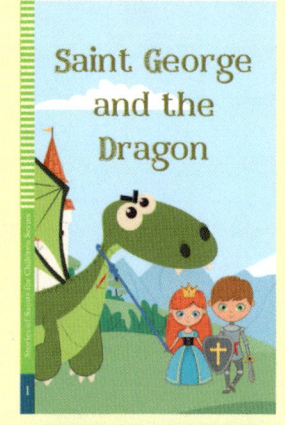

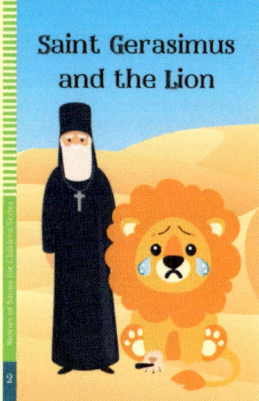

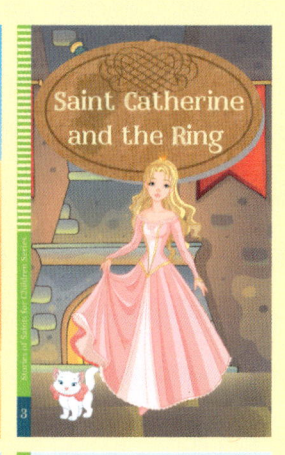

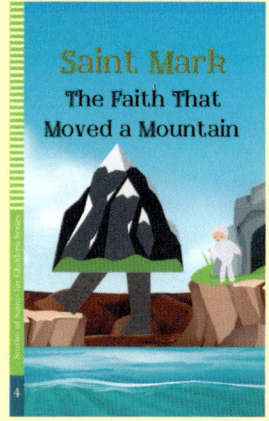

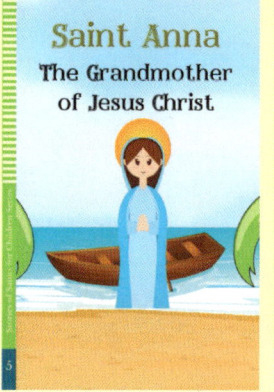

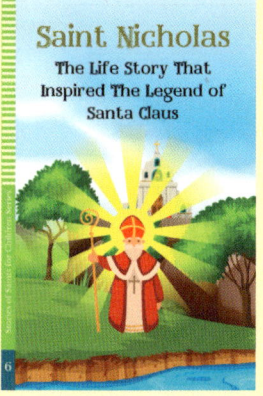

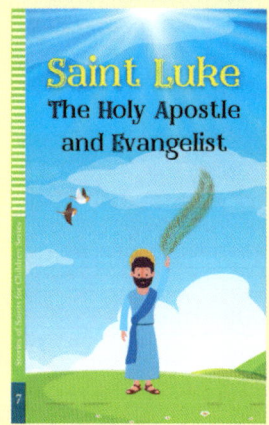

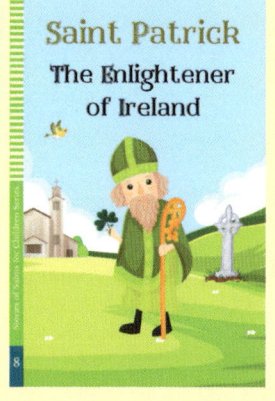

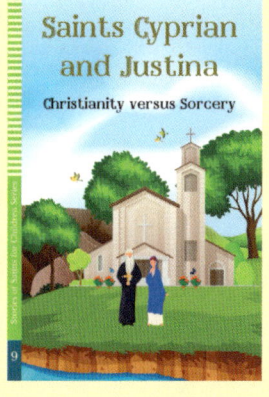

Saint George and the Dragon

Saint Gerasimus and the Lion

Saint Catherine and the Ring

Saint Mark — The Faith That Moved a Mountain

Saint Anna — The Grandmother of Jesus Christ

Saint Nicholas — The Life Story That Inspired The Legend of Santa Claus

Saint Luke — The Holy Apostle and Evangelist

Saint Patrick — The Enlightener of Ireland

Saints Cyprian and Justina — Christianity versus Sorcery

Printed in Great Britain
by Amazon